USA TODAY. **TEEN WISE GUIDES**
A GANNETT COMPANY
LIFESTYLE CHOICES

COMMUNICATION
SMARTS

How to Express Yourself Best in Conversations, Texts, E-mails, and More

SANDY DONOVAN

TWENTY-FIRST CENTURY BOOKS / MINNEAPOLIS

Twenty-First Century Books
A division of Lerner Publishing Group, Inc.
241 First Avenue North
Minneapolis, MN 55401 U.S.A.

Website address: www.lernerbooks.com

Library of Congress Cataloging-in-Publication Data

Donovan, Sandra, 1967–
        Communication smarts : how to express yourself best in conversations, texts, e-mails, and more / by Sandy Donovan.
            p. cm. — (USA TODAY teen wise guides: lifestyle choices)
        Includes bibliographical references and index.
        ISBN 978–0–7613–7024–6 (lib. bdg. : alk. paper)
            1. Oral communication—Juvenile literature. 2. Communication—Juvenile literature. I. Title.
    P95.D67 2013
    302.2—dc22   2011044269

Manufactured in the United States of America
1 – PP – 7/15/12

The images in this book are used with the permission of: © Claudia Kunin/CORBIS, p. 4; © Image Source/Getty Images, pp. 5, 55; © Sebastian Pfuetze/Digital Vision/Getty Images, p. 6; © Tetra Images/Getty Images, pp. 6-7; © Paul Grebliunas/Photodisc/ Getty Images, p. 8; The Granger Collection, New York, pp. 9, 10; © Hill Street Studios/Blend Images/Getty Images, p. 14; © Red Chopsticks/Getty Images, pp. 14-15; © Esbin-Anderson/age fotostock/Getty Images, p. 16; © JR Carvey/Streetfly Studios/Blend Images/Getty Images, p. 19; © Garrett Hubbard/USA TODAY, p. 22; © Studio 642/Blend Images/Getty Images, p. 26; © Pixellover RM 8/Alamy, pp. 26-27; © Mika/CORBIS, p. 31; © Ron Levine/Lifesize/Getty Images, p. 33; © iStockphoto.com/Andres Balcazar, p. 35; © Ana Blazic Pavlovic/Dreamstime.com, p. 36; © Haupt Aaron/Photo Researchers/Getty Images, p. 38; © Sally and Richard Greenhill/Alamy, pp. 38-39; © Monkey Business Images/The Agency Collection/Getty Images, p. 41; © KQS/Alamy, p. 43; © Jamie Grill/Getty Images, p. 44; © Dominic Chavez/The Boston Globe via Getty Images, p. 46; © Damir Cudic/The Agency Collection/ Getty Images, p. 48; © Yellow Dog Productions/The Image Bank/Getty Images, pp. 48-49; © Kevin Dodge/CORBIS, p. 52; © Yellow Dog Productions/Iconica/Getty Images, p. 53; © Sonja Pacho/CORBIS, p. 58.
Front cover: © iStockphoto.com/Diane Diederich.

Main body text set in Conduit ITC Std 11/15
Typeface provided by International Typeface Corp

CONTENTS

WHAT'S THE BIG DEAL ABOUT
Communicating?

Picture a typical day in your life. You might get up, have breakfast, argue with a sibling or two, get ready for school, and head out the door. At school, maybe you check in with a few friends, yawn your way through your morning classes, and then have lunch with your buddies—who always crack you up enough to help you make it through your afternoon classes. Then perhaps you have an after-school activity before heading home for dinner, homework, and maybe a little time online before bed.

A day without communicating would be really weird. You couldn't even joke around with your friends at lunch!

Picture that same day without any communication. Let's see: no talking with friends, family, or teachers. OK, that would be a pretty weird day. In fact, if you think about it, there would be no point in even going to school if you couldn't communicate—you couldn't have any classes. Not so bad, right? But there'd also be no Internet, no television, no phone calls, no Facebook, and no texting—not even a friendly wave to a neighbor. Hmm, this is really starting to sound like a lousy day. *Are you starting to get an idea of why communication is such a big deal?*

1 *Communication:*
FROM SPEECH AND SMOKE SIGNALS TO TEXTING AND TWITTER

You are communicating each time you send a text or give a speech in class.

*L*ike eating, sleeping, and hanging with your friends, communicating is a part of every teen's life. Every time you talk, write, type, or even look at someone, you're communicating. Some teens are natural communicators, while others struggle a bit. Maybe you're a rock star when it comes to writing, but when it comes to public speaking, you're a deer in headlights. Or maybe it's the opposite. Maybe you'd rather give a speech to a whole country than write a half-page journal entry.

When it comes to communicating, *almost everyone has room for improvement.* Keep reading to learn more about how communication affects your life, how to avoid sending mixed signals, and how to send the right message the right way.

IT'S NOTHING NEW

Communicating has been a fact of life on Earth since, well, the beginning of humankind. Historians think people started communicating with speech at least 150,000 years ago (and possibly much earlier than that). By 30,000 years ago, they were communicating with symbols, including pictures drawn on cave walls. The first alphabet soon followed. And once people had an alphabet—and a way of creating words; sentences; and long, boring books—communication really took off.

Of course, people being people, they weren't content to settle for communicating with their close neighbors. Prehistoric humans used fire to send smoke signals—the earliest known form of telecommunication, or long-distance communication. By 3000 B.C.E., most historians agree, some

This rock carving was made by American Indians more than two thousand years ago. It is an example of an early form of communication.

civilizations were using mail to send letters from place to place. Flash forward about five thousand years to the invention of electricity, and telecommunication devices started popping up all over the place. And in the past quarter century, telecommunication has changed more than in all of history before that (think cell phones, Facebook, and blogs). When it comes to communication, it's a pretty interesting time to be alive!

Alexander Graham Bell invented the first practical telephone. He is pictured here in 1876 talking into his Centennial phone.

HISTORY OF TELECOMMUNICATION TOOLS

This telegraph key from 1844 was used to produce a signal when transmitting Morse code. In Morse code, letters are represented by long and short signals of sound.

Tool	When Invented
Smoke signals	Prehistoric times
Drums	Prehistoric times
Mail	6000 B.C.E.
Hydraulic semaphore (water bucket code systems)	4000 B.C.E.
Maritime flags (flags on ships)	1500
Telegraph	1838
Telephone	1876
Radio	1896
Television	1927
World Wide Web	1980
Mobile phones	1981
E-mail	1982
Text messaging	1992
Geocities (first social networking site)	1994
AOL Instant Messenger	1997
Friendster	2002
MySpace	2003
Facebook	2004
Twitter	2006
Google+	2011

SO MANY WAYS TO COMMUNICATE, SO LITTLE TIME

It seems as if our communication options are endless. Every day, you might have several face-to-face conversations, talk on the phone, write some e-mails, post to online message boards, listen to a few classroom lectures that interest you—and a few that don't—and text and text and text. With so many options, why do you need to be good at all of it? Can't you just use all of this technology to make up for any, um, communication weaknesses you might have been born with?

In fact, you can definitely use your strength in one kind of communicating to cover up for any struggles you have in another area. But more than likely, sometimes you will need to rely on one specific kind of communicating—no matter how much you hate it.

Think of communicating as the act of delivering an idea—just like a shipping company delivers a package. The shipping company may specialize in using trucks for ground delivery, but sometimes—think oceans, jungles, and destinations on top of high hills with no paved roads—it may have to use a plane, a boat, a bicycle, a carrier pigeon, human feet, or . . . well, you get the idea.

USA TODAY Snapshots®

Are you fretting about messages?

How Wi-Fi users responded when asked how long they go before they get "antsy" about checking e-mail, instant messaging and social networking sites:

- One hour or less **47%**
- One day **46%**
- One week **7%**

Source: Impulse Research for Qwest Communications online survey of 1,063 adult Wi-Fi users in April

By Anne R. Carey and Sam Ward, USA TODAY, 2009

This USA TODAY Snapshot® shows how much Wi-Fi users relied on technology to keep in touch back in 2009. With even more people using Wi-Fi now, our reliance on technology is only growing.

USA TODAY

Money

SECTION B

MONEY.USATODAY.COM

THE NET EFFECT: EVOLUTION OR REVOLUTION?

By Kevin Maney

Is the Internet the equivalent of the invention of the printing press, or is it more like the invention of television?

Television turned out to be a powerful force that changed a lot about society. But the printing press changed everything—religion, government, science, global distribution of wealth and much more. If the Internet equals the printing press, no amount of hype could possibly overdo it.

The intriguing thing is that there's no way to really know the answer until a couple of centuries from now. Imagine asking Christopher Columbus in the 1490s whether he thought the printing press of the 1450s was as important as the invention of the alphabet.

The invention of the printing press shook every aspect of society. In religion it led to the Protestant Reformation. In government, it led to the downfall of feudalism [a social system in medieval Europe] and later made democracy possible. In business, increasing knowledge led to the Industrial Revolution.

Which brings us back to the Internet. Tim Berners-Lee is the software engineer who, while working at a lab in Geneva in 1980, created the World Wide Web. Berners-Lee's invention needed one more piece. That came from Marc Andreessen, who led the way in the development and deployment of the Web

You might be great at telling stories but start to panic at the thought of writing a letter. Unfortunately, at times you're going to have to communicate by—gasp!—letter writing.

Some of this might seem pretty basic to you. But chances are you picked up this book for a reason. Maybe you have trouble talking to new people, or maybe you want to brush up on the dos and don'ts browser in the early 1990s. By 1995, the Internet was becoming a whirlwind force. Technologies such as the PC and phone lines were in place to make the Net accessible almost anywhere, and advanced societies accepted that they had entered an Information Age—an era when information and knowledge would be among the most valuable resources.

As a world-changing invention, the Net echoes many of the characteristics of the printing press. Think of all the medical information on the Web, which, until recently, only doctors could access. Think of what you can find about cars and prices, cracking the information that had been guarded by car dealers. In those examples and many more, the Internet gives individuals more power, much as the printing press did.

The Internet also gives permanence to new levels of information. Millions of people have their own Web pages, detailing the minutia of their lives. Amazon.com publishes book reviews by individuals, not just professional reviewers, capturing what the masses think. Surf the Web, and you can find information about practically anything. There is no longer a lower limit on triviality.

And the Internet can send information to far-away places cheaply, easily and in great volume—much more than any medium before it.

There is, however, one way the Internet trumps the printing press. It is interactive. It adds a give-and-take to information that previously was possible only in person or on the phone.

—*August 9, 1999*

of writing e-mails. Maybe you're confused about when you need to write a formal letter and when a text will do. With more communication options than at any other time in history, it's easy to become overwhelmed. But take a deep breath—it's not that hard. As you learn more about the best ways to communicate, you'll probably find that communication is a lot simpler than you thought.

2 SPEAKING UP:
Good Convo

There are all kinds of conversations—from carefree to confrontational. Read on to see if your chats include the key ingredients of a good conversation.

So what exactly is a conversation? It's a spoken-word exchange of information and thoughts. Sounds simple. And really, what could be easier than having a conversation with someone? You just say something, the other person replies, you reply, and so on and so on. *Presto: conversation.*

In fact, there are all kinds of conversations. Some are simple and carefree. Others are chock-full of information, thoughts, and opinions. Some are heated or even downright confrontational. And some are sugarcoated, try-not-to-ruffle-any-feathers events. But any good conversation should include a few key ingredients. Read on to see if your typical conversations already include these ingredients or if you need a little help.

THE SPOKEN **WORD**

You can have a conversation by letter, e-mail, or even by chiseling letters into slate tablets (not recommended!). But the conversations we're talking about deal with the spoken word—the ones you have in person, over the phone, or even by video chat. So the first ingredient is—you guessed it—a dash of spoken, or verbal, language.

So what do we need to start a spoken-word conversation? How about speech? OK, maybe that's a bit obvious. But think about the type of speech you need to have. You can't just blurt out words. You have to be able to use words in a way that clearly express your thoughts. That's called being articulate. If someone asks you how school is going, they probably want to hear more than "Fine." Don't panic— you don't need to make a speech every time someone asks you a simple question. But including at least one detail—and putting that thought into a complete sentence—is a great start. For instance: "School's going great right now. I have a new science teacher, and she's really making biology interesting." Not so hard, right?

Of course, you do also have to pay attention to how you pronounce the words you say. Think about it: would you rather have a conversation with someone who says, "Hey, I saw an absolutely awesome movie yesterday—it's called *Attack of the Abominable Alligator*" or "Hey, I saw anabsu lu-au movie yesseray—call Atta uhtheah Bomb Nibbleaguh"?

It's easy to see how *being articulate is an important aspect of speaking*. After that, you just need to worry about three small details when speaking: volume, tone, and inflection. Let's look at those one by one.

VOLUME

Volume is the loudness of your words. You need to speak loudly enough to be heard but not so loud as to be, well, deafening. And of course, volume will depend largely on the situation. If you're communicating an urgent message to a teammate on the soccer field, yelling might be appropriate. If you're working with a friend on a research paper in the public library, anything more than a whisper might earn you a dirty look.

TECHNOLOGY
LEAVES TEENS SPEECHLESS

By Olivia Barker

To be sure, the monthly bills—as high as $300—were a problem.

But there were other, audible consequences of the fact that Alexandra Smith would pound out more than 1,000 text messages from her cell phone a month: She was chatting—constantly, exhaustively—but she wasn't talking. It got so that Smith's parents were begging her to put the phone to her lips instead of her fingertips.

So these days Smith, 18, is practicing something that came oh-so-naturally to tides of teens before her: the art of vocal gab. Instead of holing up at home and punching out digital dialogue, Smith is making an effort to actually meet up with her three best friends and flex her throat muscles.

"I figured I should probably go over and learn how to talk to somebody," says the Eugene, Oregon, high school senior. "I didn't want to be the dork at college who texts all the time."

She needn't worry. College suitemates, even roommates, pick up their phones to ping each other. Otherwise, they're communicating via instant messaging or social networking sites.

With their mouths largely shut but their laptops and flip phones open, teenagers' bedrooms are beginning to sound like the library. Not long ago, prattling away on the phone was as much a teenage rite as hanging out at the mall. Flopped on the bed, you yakked into your pink or football-shaped receiver until your parents hollered at you to get off.

Now, conversations, the oral kind, are as uncomfortable as braces. Which makes employers and communications experts anxious: This generation may be technologically savvier than their bosses, but will they be able to have a professional discussion?

"We are losing very natural, human, instinctive skills that we used to be really good at," says Sonya Hamlin, author of *How to Talk So People Listen: Connecting in Today's Workplace.*

Some teens don't have enough practice speaking to people because of the amount of time they spend texting. This can become a problem in future college and job interviews.

A couple of years ago, Hamlin was asked to teach a class of "very bright" California high school seniors about the college admissions interview. Their mock answers were "extremely short and not informational. Nothing came out, really, because it's such an unused skill."

Part of the reason, Hamlin says, is because "they're not listening. With IM, you can reread six times before deciding how to answer." Stefani Beser, a freshman at Villa Julie College near Baltimore, texts so much that the shorthand creeps into her live conversation. "You'll be talking and all of sudden you'll say, 'Oh, LOL,' text-speak for "laughing out loud."

—*May 30, 2006*

YOUR MOST IMPORTANT CONVERSATION

Have you ever interviewed for a job? A job interview is really just a type of conversation. These Q&A sessions can seem scary, and it's true that often they're a bit one-sided, but they're also super important. Want to buy a car someday or pay for your college education? Then you'd better be prepared to nail this particular type of conversation!

Employers who interview teens for jobs say they don't expect them to be as polished as an adult. But they do want you to be able to hold your own. Check out this list of tips for job interviews. They just might help you land the job you've been wanting!

- Look at the interviewer, not the ground, your hands, or the clock.
- Show that you have done some research. Mention something positive about the specific job or the company.
- Come prepared with a list of questions about the job or the company.
- Display interest and enthusiasm about the job.
- Dress neatly.
- Thank the interviewer for his or her time at the end of the interview.
- Smile!

Top skills for new hires

Here's what employers identified as the most important skills, along with what recent college graduates said they believe employers most value. (Respondents were asked to identify the two most important skills.)

■ Employers ■ Recent graduates

Teamwork
- 44%
- 38%

Critical thinking/reasoning
- 33%
- 37%

Oral/written communication
- 30%
- 37%

Source: Peter D. Hart Research Associates based on surveys of 305 business leaders and 510 recent college graduates Nov. 2-Dec. 5, 2006

By Karl Gelles, USA TODAY, 2007

This USA TODAY Snapshot® shows what job skills employers valued in 2006 versus what skills young job seekers thought

TONE

Tone refers to the way spoken words can reflect the speaker's feelings or opinions. If you're excited about something, your tone may be sort of high and edgy or you may speak quickly and more loudly. If you're angry about something, your words may take on a sharp or harsh tone. Happiness, fear, sadness, curiosity, disbelief, and many more feelings can be reflected by tone. Tone can change the entire meaning of a sentence. Don't believe that? Think about the way a mother would say, "I can't believe you did that!" to a kid who just broke a window. Now think about the way that same mother would say those same words to a kid who just got the highest grade in her class. The difference is in tone—and in this case, it carries as much meaning as the words themselves.

INFLECTION

Finally, a speaker's inflection also carries a lot of weight in a conversation. Inflection is the way a speaker voices his or her words, including which words are stressed. Inflection is a lot like tone, but it specifically means to use a change in the sound of your voice to convey meaning. The most common inflection in the English language is the little upward inflection used at the end of a question. During this upward inflection, the speaker's voice goes into a higher pitch, like a singer reaching a higher note. Say a few questions out loud, and you'll quickly get the idea.

MIND YOUR MANNERS

You've probably heard the expression "Say it, don't spray it," right? It's just a little reminder to follow basic manners when you're speaking.

Yes, being polite is another necessary ingredient to a good conversation. Hopefully it goes without saying that you shouldn't spit on your conversation partner. But you might be surprised to know just how often people forget the most basic conversation manners.

Most conversation manners are pretty basic. Still, it can be easy to forget them—especially when you're shy, confused, or just not interested in the conversation. Check out a few basic rules below, and think about whether you need to improve on any of these areas.

- Make eye contact—both when you're speaking and when you're listening.
- Don't interrupt when somebody is in the middle of a thought.
- Answer questions with more than one word—especially if that word is "Yeah," or "Iguessso" or "Idunno."
- Smile when you're having a conversation.
- Ask questions.

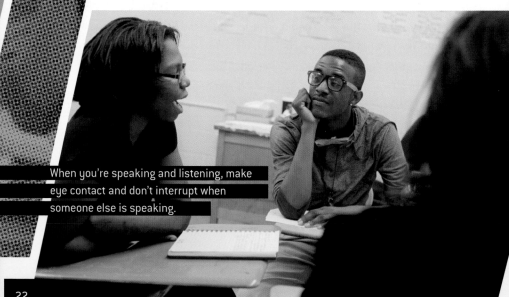

When you're speaking and listening, make eye contact and don't interrupt when someone else is speaking.

NONVERBAL CLUES: WHAT'S YOUR BODY SAYING

In most conversations, your body language can convey as much meaning as your words. Think about these different types of body language and how you can use them to improve any conversation.

- **Eye contact.** Maintaining eye contact is the best way to show you're interested and engaged in a conversation. Looking people in the eye makes them feel more connected to you, and they'll be more likely to be interested in the conversation as well.
- **Smile.** A smile is a great way to get any conversation off to a good start. If you're in a one-on-one conversation, your smile will put the other person at ease. And in a group conversation, you'll be more likely to be included and listened to if you have a smile—and a positive attitude to go with it.
- **Hand gestures.** Many people find that using their hands during a conversation is helpful. Simple gestures can help to give your words emphasis. This comes naturally to some people. Others have to work at it. Just be careful not to overdo it. And remember that except with close friends and family, most people aren't excited to be touched by a conversation partner. On the other hand, gestures such as crossing your arms or burying your hands in your pockets can send the signal that you're bored by a conversation.
- **Your posture.** The way you stand says a lot about how you feel about a conversation. Stand up straight and face the people you're talking to so you show that you care.

ADD A LITTLE
BACK-AND-FORTH

The last ingredient to a successful conversation is a splash of back-and-forth. Remember the definition of a conversation from the beginning of this chapter? It's an *exchange* of information and thoughts. That means more than one person needs to be speaking. You shouldn't be doing all the speaking, and you shouldn't be doing all the listening either. That's called a lecture, not a conversation!

Of course, some conversations are a bit one-sided. If you're telling a friend about your recent vacation, for example, you'll probably be doing most of the talking. But even so, there should be some back-and-forth going on. Otherwise, your audience is likely to get bored by it all. Imagine this conversation:

> Then I looked up and all of a sudden the biggest wave I've ever seen was crashing down over my head. I had no idea what I was going to do. Man, I started thinking, is this it? Am I never coming out of this ocean alive? I started flashing back to my family, thinking about all kinds of things. Wow, it seemed like it was all going by in such a blur. So anyway, there I was, with this wave crashing down on me.

At this point, it doesn't really matter what you say next—your listener probably stopped listening about three sentences ago. By now, she's thinking about that movie she watched last night, what she's going to have for dinner, and maybe even hoping a giant wave will come crashing down to spare her the rest of your story. It's not that she didn't want to hear about your vacation. She just wasn't expecting to have to listen to such a drawn-out account.

How do you save this conversation? Simple. *You invite her to speak!* You could simply pause and give her a chance. Or you could ask questions during your story. Imagine the same scene but with a different approach:

> *"Then I looked up and all of a sudden the biggest wave I've ever seen was crashing down over my head. You can probably imagine what that felt like. Have you ever had that feeling of absolute panic before?"*
>
> Then your friend might say, *"Oh yeah, I remember once flying so fast down a hill on my bike. I wasn't sure how I was going to survive."*
>
> *"So you know what I mean. Luckily for me, I didn't have to crash to avoid the wave—I just ducked and held my breath."*

Just by adding a simple question, you've engaged your friend. By taking the time to listen to her comment and respond to it, you've acknowledged that she's got something valuable to say too. You've made your conversation more interesting—and enjoyable.

And when it comes down to it, enjoyment is a major goal of most conversations. A conversation means that two or more people are exchanging information and ideas. But more than that, a conversation is a social event. When you have a conversation, you're building a relationship, making a new friend, enjoying an old friend, sharing your opinion, or just taking part in your community. You don't need a fascinating topic to make a conversation. You just need a few key ingredients: speaking skills, manners, and the ability to engage in a little back-and-forth.

3 Texting and More: COMMUNICATING IN THE TWENTY-FIRST CENTURY

Remember, manners and etiquette matter just as much in texting and online conversations as they do when you're chatting face-to-face.

So it's the twenty-first century. You probably carry out as many conversations by text, e-mail, or Facebook messages as you do in person. It may sometimes seem as if all you ever do is send texts. After all, teens send more texts than any other group in the United States. A 2011 study found that kids ages twelve to seventeen sent an average of 3,364 texts per month! And of course, texting isn't the only mobile way that teens communicate with their friends. The same study found that nearly 80 percent of twelve- to seventeen-year-olds used blogs or social networking sites such as Facebook to keep up with their friends. Put it all together and *that's a lot of typing!*

PLUGGED IN BUT TUNED OUT?

By Greg Toppo

Being a friend of Chandler DeWitt's means never having to say "Where are you?"

The freshman at North Carolina's High Point University says she and her friends have "six or seven ways" to get in touch most days: cell phone, texting, instant messaging, e-mail, Facebook, Twitter and Skype videoconferencing.

"I'm probably on my computer four hours out of the day, doing different stuff for school or talking to people," says DeWitt, 18, who, for all her connectivity, turns out to be a "light" media user: A new survey from the Kaiser Family Foundation finds that kids [spent] more than 7½ hours a day with electronic media [in 2009], up from about six hours in 1999.

Most young people have a cell phone and an iPod—and nearly one in three own a laptop computer.

Omead Kohanteb, 18, a freshman at the University of California-Berkeley, says Facebook and cell phones have made it easy for him to fit in on campus and make friends. He estimates that 99 percent of students have cell phones: "Everyone I've met has one."

Just because you're typing instead of speaking doesn't mean that all the rules of conversation go out the window. *Manners and etiquette still matter!* Keep reading to get a better sense of what you should—and shouldn't—do when communicating this way.

TO TEXT OR NOT TO TEXT?

No doubt about it—teens like to text. What could be better than the chance to instantly connect to your friends? No matter where your

But media can just as easily create a wall, says 14-year-old Morgan. She has an iPod loaded with her favorite bands and says popping in earbuds while she's riding the school bus is the perfect way to tell people to, in so many words, Go away.

"It's 6 a.m. and you don't want anybody bothering you," she says. "People know not to talk to you."

The media/happiness connection "makes a lot of sense to me, actually," she says. Kids who seem more isolated are "way into their music and all that kind of stuff."

But just because young people listen to a lot of music doesn't mean they're unhappy, she says. "I'll always just keep my music on while I'm studying or doing my homework."

"There has to be a balance," says Paul Caputo, a father of three boys in Ashland, Pennsylvania. "Technology is great, but the balance is that you need to have face-to-face communication. You need to maintain relationships beyond a computer screen or text message."

—*January 20, 2010*

friend is, you can ask a question, make a funny comment, or send a warning with the simple tap of a few fingers.

If you're a texter, you probably don't need any help with the basics of how to text—it's not rocket science after all. But what *can* get complicated is knowing when it's appropriate to text. Ask yourself two questions before you start tapping away: Is this the appropriate time and place for texting? Is texting the appropriate method for the conversation I want to have? Let's take a look at both of these questions.

First, how do you know when it's appropriate to text? There are some obvious times and places where texting is definitely not cool. Driving and texting is of course not only megadangerous but also illegal in most states. And

USA TODAY Snapshots®

Why texting makes us :-)

Reasons people say they like texting on cellphones:

Convenient for basic information	79%
Works where talking won't do	75%
Quicker than calling	56%
Easier when facing arguments	37%
Dislike phone conversations	27%
Great for flirting	25%

Source: GfK Roper for Best Buy Mobile survey of 1,000 adults

By Anne R. Carey and Gwen Saunders, USA TODAY, 2009

This USA TODAY Snapshot® from 2009 sheds light on why so many of us can't get enough of texting—and texting has dramatically increased in popularity since 2009!

texting during class is usually forbidden. Your parents or other adults may have rules about texting at the dinner table or other family times.

But what about those not-so-black-and-white moments? Is it OK to answer a really important text from one friend when you're having lunch with another friend? Is it cool to send a quick text when you're with a group, but they're talking about something you're not really interested in? What if you're having dinner at your friend's house but suddenly remember that you were supposed to text your mom to tell her where you are? Are any of those times the right time to text? The answer is no, no, and no. And the reason is simple: it's never OK to text with someone else when you're in the middle of a conversation or gathering with others. It's like telling the people that you're with that they're not very important to you. If you do really need to send a text at such a time, the only polite way to do it is to say, "Excuse me for a moment. I just realized I forgot to tell my mom where I am and need to send her a quick text."

Now let's think about the second question. When is texting the right way to communicate? Punching out a quick text to ask a friend what he's doing after school may be perfectly acceptable. But texting your new boss to say that you can't come to work that day isn't.

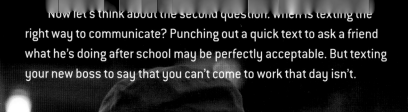

Use texting to communicate simple stuff with friends and family.

Why not? Because texting is a very informal way to communicate. It's for light, easy stuff with friends and family. It's not for serious topics, and it's not ideal for people you don't really know well.

Think about a couple of examples. First, would you text your new boss to ask what time you are supposed to show up on your first day or work? No! This is a conversation to have in person, by phone, or even by e-mail. You want your new boss to know that you take things like showing up for work on time seriously. A text is too informal to give this message. For the same reason, you probably wouldn't text your friend to tell her you're sorry that her close family member died. Again, you want your friend to know that this is important to you. Expressing that thought in person, in a letter, on the phone, or even by e-mail might make it seem more sincere.

Keep these simple things in mind when you're texting. It's a great way to communicate, but you have to remember when and where it's appropriate.

E-MAIL

E-mail is a lot like texting. It's a super-easy way to talk to people anywhere at any time. In fact, for adults, it's the most common form of communication. It's still less formal than a written letter but more formal than a text. So as you've probably guessed, e-mailing comes with a few more etiquette rules.

First thing's first. When e-mailing, follow the basic rules of writing—that includes spelling, grammar, and punctuation. Imagine this: You're getting ready for a job interview, but you need directions to the company's office. You could knock out an e-mail as if you're texting a friend:

Hi, where r u at? Can u send directions?

Or you could send a more formal e-mail with a greeting, a closing, and no texting abbreviations:

Dear Mr. Smith:

I'm scheduled to interview with you at 3 P.M. this afternoon, but I'm having trouble locating your office. Could you please send me directions?

Thank you,
[Your Name]

One of those e-mails is going to make a better impression before you even meet Mr. Smith—and you can probably guess which one it is. Every e-mail you send doesn't need to be a literary masterpiece, but you should take the time to read through each one before you hit Send—and don't forget that *spell-check is your friend!*

Another key thing to keep in mind when e-mailing is that you don't have the benefit of nonverbal clues. Remember them?

Don't forget to check your grammar, spelling, and punctuation before sending an e-mail.

YOUR E-MAIL ADDRESS SAYS A LOT!

Lots of teens spend time thinking up cute or clever e-mail addresses (think PartyGuy2012@whatever.com or CutieGirl@something.com). But few stop to think how these addresses will look in the eyes of the adults in their lives. The fact is that cute or, even worse, offensive e-mail names can cost you the good opinion of many adults. And if you're unwise enough to use one when applying for a job, it can cost you the job as well. Before you e-mail an important adult, make sure your address is appropriate. Not sure if it is? Ask an adult you trust. If it isn't, take the few minutes needed to register for a free Web-based account. Sites such as Google and Yahoo are popular for free online e-mail accounts.

They're the facial expressions, tone of voice, eye contact, gestures, and other actions that help communicate meaning in an in-person conversation. So clarity is crucial. *Be direct and straightforward.* Don't leave any room for misunderstanding. It's best to avoid sarcasm (humor that states the opposite of your true meaning) and jokes that could be misinterpreted. A good rule is that if you're uncertain whether the person reading your e-mail will get your joke, leave it out.

Hopefully you're beginning to see a common thread in all this e-mail etiquette. The best general rule for e-mailing is to write carefully, reread, and think twice before sending e-mails. Even though you can send a dozen e-mails in practically the blink of an eye, each one can make a huge impression on whoever's inbox it ends up in.

One more thing to keep in mind when e-mailing is your own emotional state. If you just had a fight with your best friend, don't fire off a nasty e-mail filled with accusations. Once you hit Send, you can't get that e-mail back. A good rule of thumb is to wait an hour—or even a day—and reread your e-mail before sending it. When you've calmed down a bit, you might realize that some things simply don't need to be said at all.

SOCIAL MEDIA

So what about online social media sites? Are there even rules for Facebook, Twitter, and similar sites? *You bet there are!* Think about it: social media sites are like an ongoing, public conversation with everybody you're friends with. A lot of teens tweet about every moment of their day or share *everything* with their Facebook friends. Had a delicious muffin for breakfast? Why not post a photo? A killer math test? Post a quick complaint and see the sympathies of your friends come rolling in as comments. What could be easier than keeping everyone you know updated about your every move?

But do you stop and think about all the people who see these posts? If you're Facebook friends with four hundred people, then all four hundred of those friends may see your every update.

GUARD YOUR ONLINE IMAGE

You probably wouldn't act inappropriately—use bad language or make offensive comments—around your teachers, bosses, or friends' parents . . . right? But did you know that those same people might be able to see almost anything you post online? That's right. A simple search engine check can pop up photos, comments, and other stuff you've posted. So before you post rude comments, revealing photos, or evidence of inappropriate behavior, think about who might see it.

Think you're safe because you've password-protected your Facebook and other social media sites? Check it out by doing a quick Google search on yourself. You might be surprised at what pops up: many search engines results include content posted on password-protected sites.

Before you post revealing photos or evidence of inappropriate behavior, think about who might see it—such as teachers or bosses.

Is that OK? Think about this situation: you're at an awesome party, but one of your close friends wasn't invited. You're thinking about posting a few great photos to show how much fun you're having. But your friend who didn't get invited will probably see them. You'd never even think of calling your friend just to tell her how awesome the party is. That would make her feel bad. But posting photos is almost the same thing. Or maybe you're friends with your grandmother, and you're not sure she'd approve of your being out so late. You've got to remember all the people who will see your post and how it will affect them.

Privacy and safety are also big concerns. Depending on your account settings, even friends of friends may be able to see your photos and read your posts. That can include a lot of people you don't know. Some posts can actually put you in danger. Photos could draw the attention of sexual predators. Or criminals could find information on you to steal your identity or worse. Think about this situation. Your family is leaving for a weeklong vacation. Posting that info for strangers to read could be like posting a big fat invitation to a burglar. The lesson here is to remember to consider all the people who might see your post and what they might do with that information. Check out account settings and know how far your information is going to travel. If you're at all unsure of whether to post something, it's better to be cautious. *Don't take any chances.*

4 Letter Writing: AN OLD-FASHIONED ART?

Letter writing isn't as popular as it once was. But it's still an important skill to have.

$\mathcal{S}$ure, you know all about talking, texting, and e-mailing—but have you ever heard of a galaxy far, far away where cell phones, the Internet, instant messaging, and even—*gasp!*—Facebook—don't exist? OK, maybe that's a bit dramatic. You know you don't have to travel to another galaxy to find such a civilization. All you need is a time machine that can go back about twenty years.

So how exactly did people communicate in those dark ages? Believe it or not, they actually wrote letters! With pens and pencils or maybe even typewriters. And they stuck them in envelopes, pasted stamps on them, and dropped them in the mailbox. Curious, indeed. But is this anything that you really need to know about? You bet! Letters are not a thing of the past. We don't use them as often these days, but they do still have a place—and you need to know when to use them and how to write them.

WRITING A WRONG:
TOO MANY STUDENTS CAN'T PUT PEN—OR PENCIL—TO PAPER

By Laura Vanderkam

Ariel Horn is reaping praise these days for her first novel, *Help Wanted, Desperately*. But the writing feedback she remembers most wasn't a review. It was a letter, "B+" specifically, on a paper her junior year in high school.

"I was indignant!" she says. "How could my teacher not recognize my literary genius?"

Perhaps, the teacher noted, it was because her genius lay buried beneath grammatical woes. Horn rewrote the essay—and, "I have flashbacks of that B+ paper," she says.

Horn now teaches English in a Manhattan public school. Her students, too, revise papers multiple times as Horn advises their grammar and style. With 100-plus students, "I am personally in grading [misery]," she says. But her charges do learn to write.

Unfortunately, studies suggest that they're part of a small, lucky crew. As high school seniors race to meet December college-application deadlines, most face the oft-required "personal statement" with understandable dread. Only a quarter of America's 12th-graders, the 2002 National Assessment of Educational Progress found, can write tolerable essays. Only about 2 percent create the kind of zesty prose that makes reading worthwhile.

The well-financed among the rest hire editing services and zoom to the top of the college admissions pile. Meanwhile, schools that fail to teach writing face few consequences. For three years [as of 2004], the federal No Child Left Behind Act (NCLB) has held schools to strict reading and arithmetic standards. But the law [was] strangely quiet about the third "R" of the trio.

Why stop at two of three R's? Holding schools accountable for teaching kids to write will both level the college playing field and give students a job skill they deserve.

A recent survey of corporate America by the National Commission on Writing

Employers and college administrators will expect you to be able to write clearly. That's a pretty good reason to pay attention in English class!

found clear prose is a resume must. "In most cases, writing ability could be your ticket in . . . or it could be your ticket out," one human resources (HR) director notes. Yet, "people's writing skills are not where they need to be," another says. Cover letters sag with needless words, fuzzy logic and grammatical mistakes. Ask college admissions counselors about application essays, and they list the same sins.

Not every classroom can be like Horn's, where students learn grammar by day and hear the teacher read her fiction at Barnes & Noble by night. But all students deserve the tools to make their ideas understood. As one HR director told the National Commission on Writing, "Applicants who provide poorly written letters likely wouldn't get an interview."

Schools fail students headed to college and the job market when they let poor writing slide.

—*December 1, 2004*

Remember at the beginning of this book when we mentioned that your audience—who you are communicating with—should determine the method you use? Well, there are lots of times when a letter is simply the most appropriate way to communicate. It's always great to send a letter home from camp, drop a note in the mail to your grandma, or even write a twenty-page missive to your best friend. But most teens need to know how to write letters to two main audiences. In a nutshell, they are gift givers and future bosses. Sounds like odd company. But think about what gift givers and future bosses have in common. When somebody is thoughtful enough to give you a gift, you want to show that you value it. And when somebody is considering hiring you for a job, you also want to show that you value the opportunity.

So what's a better way to show someone you value something—to quickly tap out a text, or to go to the trouble of finding a card or a sheet of paper, writing a few complete sentences, and sealing and addressing your thoughts in an envelope? If you

USA TODAY Snapshots®

Fewer letters being mailed

The U.S. Postal Service, facing increasing competition, saw mail volume drop 9.5 billion pieces last fiscal year — the biggest drop ever.

Mail volume, in billions:

202.2 213.1 202.7

'03 '04 '05 '06 '07 '08

Note: Statistics tabulated for fiscal years

Source: U.S. Postal Service

By Anne R. Carey and Alejandro Gonzalez, USA TODAY, 2009

This USA TODAY Snapshot® shows that mailing letters was growing less common even back in 2008. It's even more uncommon these days—but that doesn't mean you're off the hook! You'll probably still have to mail a letter in many situations.

guessed texting, guess again. Sometimes an old-fashioned letter is the only way to go. *Argh*, you might groan, *do I really have to do all that work when I could just send a quick text?* Unfortunately, yes, sometimes you do. But the good news is that it really doesn't have to be all that much work. Let's take a look at the two most common types of letters teens should know how to write.

THANK-YOU NOTES

The time-honored thank-you note remains the best way to express thanks for a gift or good deed. Notice that these are called thank-you notes and not thank-you letters—that's because they really don't have to be literary masterpieces. They simply have to *express your appreciation* for what you've received. The best and most meaningful part about a thank-you note is that you wrote one. That takes the pressure off the content (the actual words you write).

In fact, a thank-you note can be a very simple affair. There are just a few key steps:

1. **Find paper.** This can be anything from fancy, embossed, and personalized stationery cards to a clean sheet of loose-leaf paper. The only rule is that the paper should be clean and neat—don't scrawl a note on an old receipt you found in your pocket or on the back of last week's math assignment.

You can use stationery cards or just a clean sheet of loose leaf to write your thank-you note.

THANK YOU!

2. Begin with a personal salutation. (That's a fancy word for greeting.) This is probably the most formal part of the thank-you note, and it's about two words long. (See, thank-you notes aren't as scary as you might think!). Using someone's name adds a lot to a note. So instead of writing "Hey, . . ." try, "Dear Aunt Mabel, . . ."

3. **Say thanks.** Seems pretty obvious, right? It is. This is the meat of your note, and all you have to do is write something as obvious as, "Thank you for the gift card you sent for my birthday."

4. **Add something nice.** OK, here's the trickiest part of a thank-you note—and it's really not that tricky. After you write a sentence saying "thank you," you just add a few personal comments. You could say something you really like about the gift: "Vanilla-tangerine-almond is my absolute favorite soap scent." You could say something about how you hope to use a gift card: "I'll definitely have fun picking out a book to spend this gift card on." You could say something you really like about the gift giver: "It was great to see you at my birthday dinner." . . . Well, you get the idea.

5. **Sign your name.** Yes, it's really that simple! Once you've written a few sentences, you can simply add "Sincerely, James" or "Thanks again, Sasha." Pretty painless, right?

THE ALL-IMPORTANT
COVER LETTER

A cover letter—a letter you send along with your résumé when you're applying for a job—may be one of the most important letters you'll ever write. Like the thank-you note, it might seem left over from a bygone era, but the cover letter is alive and well in today's business culture. We're discussing cover letters in this chapter about paper-and-pencil letters, because the traditional medium for a cover letter is paper. But if you're applying for a job online and especially if you're e-mailing your résumé to apply for a job, you'll likely craft an electronic cover letter.

A counselor looks over a student's cover letter for a job application. Proofreading your cover letter is very important.

Like thank-you notes, cover letters can be easier to write than you might think. That's because they follow a pretty standard format. Check out the example on the opposite page to get an idea of what to include in your cover letter and how to present it.

Once you've got the basic format down, the only thing to remember is to *proofread, proofread, and proofread.* That's right—*three* proofreads! Nothing turns off a potential employer more than a sloppy cover letter. Save your job prospects by using the Proof x3 method: The first time, ask a friend or an adult with good writing skills to read it over and give you suggestions. The second time, use spell-check and grammar-check on your computer to find any obvious mistakes. For the final proof, print out a copy and read it slowly, out loud, to yourself. Don't send it in until you feel confident you've got it right.

COVER LETTER EXAMPLE

Your name
Street address
City, state, and zip code
Phone number
E-mail address

Date

Recipient's name
Recipient's job title
Name of business
Street address
City, state, and zip code

Dear Mr./Ms._____:

Introduction. State your interest in the specific job or type of work you're applying for. Mention how you learned about the job opening.

Sales pitch. Say exactly why you would be great at this job. Be specific about how your skills and/or experience make you the best candidate for the job. Explain why you have chosen to apply for this particular job.

Strong closing. Say that you'd like to meet with the employer. Be sure to describe your plan to follow up (you'll call next week, etc.). Mention that your résumé is enclosed. Include day and evening contact information, even though it is also listed at the top of the letter. Finally, thank the employer for his or her time.

Sincerely,
[Your signature goes here, unless submitting electronically.]

5 COMMUNICATION SKILLS
Use 'Em or Lose 'Em

Communication skills are pretty basic, but read on to see how to take your communication skills even further.

*I*f you've made it this far, you should have a pretty good handle on how to carry on conversations, communicate online, and even write a good old-fashioned letter. And you may have realized that no matter what the method—in-person, phone, letter, etc.—communication skills are fairly basic. You might even be thinking that you've got this all down and you're ready to go be an expert communicator.

Well, not so fast. It's true that every teen is a communicator. But there really is a difference between just getting by and being a *great* communicator. You know that kid at school who won't stop talking about how great he is? And how just about everybody tries to avoid him? That kid may be communicating, but he's not a great communicator— or he would have noticed that people are avoiding him. And what about that kid who always gives one-word answers and barely looks at anyone she's talking to? She's probably naturally reserved. But being reserved doesn't prevent you from being a great communicator.

GIVE AND GAIN:
IT'S A TWO-WAY STREET

Great communicators come in all personalities, sizes, and ages. But one thing they all know is that communicating is not only about getting *their* ideas across. They know that learning about other people, places, and things is every bit as important.

For instance, think about this quick question: what's the absolute, hands-down best tool you have for gaining knowledge or understanding a situation? (Hint: the answer is the topic of this book.) *Yep, communication.* It's your number one tool for gathering information. Don't be afraid to use it!

The major ingredients of communication etiquette apply. Be articulate, polite, and engage in back-and-forth. Don't be afraid to *politely* speak up and ask questions. Maybe you didn't hear the final turn in a list of directions or you feel as if you've missed the entire point of a history class lecture.

USA TODAY Snapshots®

Open to misinterpretation

Communication modes that adults find easy to misinterpret the tone:

Mode	Percent
E-mail	80%
Text message	78%
Letter/written	71%
Telephone	53%
Face-to-face	37%

Source: Harris Interactive survey for Whitepages.com of 2,395 adults Jan. 3–Jan. 5. Margin of error, ±3 percentage points. Respondents could answer more than one

By Mary Cadden and Suzy Parker, USA TODAY, 2007

Clarity in communication is a big deal. This USA TODAY Snapshot® shows which forms of communication are the most likely to be misinterpreted according to survey takers in 2007.

MIXED SIGNALS

Communicating might seem straightforward. But often, it's not as simple as it seems. Spoken, written, and online communication are all prime candidates for being misinterpreted, or taken the wrong way. Have you ever fumed for days over something your friend said—only to find out later that she didn't really mean what you thought you heard at all? Or maybe you've received an e-mail that was meant to be a joke—only you took it as real, and it really hurt your feelings. If you've ever texted, you've more than likely typed a few wrong letters—and completely changed the meaning of your message. The point is that sometimes the message we mean to send just isn't the one that the other person receives. And that's a problem.

Misinterpretation will always be a part of communication. Sometimes the result is funny. Autocorrect on smartphones provides lots of laughs. Have you heard about the teen who texted her friend that she went blind? That friend told all their other friends, and everyone was really worried about their newly blind friend. But at school the next day, they were surprised and relieved to see that she really went *blonde*, not blind. Of course, sometimes the results of mixed signals aren't so funny. Hurt feelings can linger even after the misinterpretation is cleared up.

Naturally, people don't want to hurt one another's feelings. So it's important to try to review your communicating style and message whenever you get the chance. Sometimes this is really simple, like reading over a text or an e-mail before you hit Send. Other times, you may want to take a look at your body language—a mirror can work for this—to see what messages you're sending along with your words. For extra delicate or ultra-important messages, you can even practice your delivery on a friend or a family member beforehand.

Conflict between people comes up all the time. These teens could solve their issues in a healthy way by talking out their problems.

Nothing can help you more than communicating your questions, asking for clarity, and verifying—making sure you understand—the answer. Don't go through life confused or misunderstood because you didn't speak up!

SETTLE DIFFERENCES

Conflict comes up almost every day in a teen's life. Maybe you argue with your parents over curfew times. Maybe you find yourself fighting with a friend or a classmate for reasons you don't even really understand. Or maybe you just can't get along with the new guy where you work. Whatever the source, conflict is an inevitable part of life. It turns out that the best way to resolve conflict is with a healthy dose of communication.

The first step in most conflict resolution is to talk it out. Maybe the other person doesn't even realize there's a problem. Or maybe there's a simple misunderstanding. In conflict resolution, the back-and-forth of conversation is especially important. Make your opinion known. But also listen. You can't resolve the conflict until you understand the other person's viewpoint. You don't have to agree with it, but you need to understand it.

Also remember that during a conflict, emotions can run high. Don't let them get the better of you! You can keep things calm by using "I" statements rather than "you" statements. Take this example: Your best friend threw a party and didn't invite you. You could say, "You hurt me," or you could say, "I felt hurt." See the difference? They convey the same message. But with the "I" statement, it doesn't sound like blaming. That sort of statement is less likely to make your friend feel defensive. It's just one example of carefully choosing your words. Check out the list below for a few more quick tips on resolving a conflict.

- Discuss the issue directly with the person(s) involved.
- Address conflict early. If you have a difference of opinion with someone, ask him or her politely if you can talk about it. Ask if now or a later time is convenient.
- Keep calm.
- Be respectful.

Staying calm and being respectful while attempting to resolve a conflict can help you and your friend get back on good terms.

- Listen actively (try to understand the other person's point of view).
- Focus on the problem, not the person.
- Find ways to move past your differences. Agree on what you have in common and agree to disagree if necessary.

LET IT SHINE!

Ever had to stand up in front of a group of people and give a public speech? If you're like many teens, you might prefer to slowly tear off your toenails. But you'll probably have to give a speech a few times in your life—as a student, at your job, or even at your best friend's wedding someday. And while few people are born good public speakers, almost everybody can gain the skills to become a confident public speaker.

Check out this list of public speaking tips to get you started:

1. Prepare. Do your research and make note cards with key phrases and ideas, not complete sentences.
2. Practice, practice, and practice. Practice to your mom. Practice to your mirror. Practice to your dog. Then do it again. And again. Are you getting the idea?
3. Dress for success. You don't have to get all gussied up, but looking your best—and appropriate for the situation—will make you feel more confident.
4. Visualize yourself being fabulous. Thinking about how great you're going to be can actually help you be great.
5. Relax. Public speaking is a big deal, but it's not the biggest thing ever. The worst that can happen is you'll make a few mistakes—and if you do, chances are, no one will even notice.
6. Slow down. Talking too fast is the number one mistake of nervous people. You can actually calm yourself down by slowing down.

7. **Look at your audience.** Make eye contact with a few different people in the audience, and stand up straight. The number one sign of confidence is holding your head up straight.
8. **Add a little humor.** It helps to keep everyone engaged and relaxed at the same time. But don't overdo it or use inappropriate humor.
9. **Smile.** It'll make others feel as if they're enjoying themselves too.
10. **Use the underwear tactic.** OK, you don't really have to picture your audience in their underwear. But who knows? It might just help you!

With a little practice, you'll find that you can apply the communication skills you've learned to almost any situation. You'll be on your way to gaining information, sharing information, and resolving conflicts with a lot more ease and confidence!

If you have to give a speech in front of your class, be prepared, smile, and look at your audience.

HEY, WALLFLOWERS: LEARN TO START A CONVERSATION WITH EASE; AND FIND OUT WHAT NOT TO SAY

By Jaime Sarrio and Emily Bazar

Debra Fine, author of *The Fine Art of Small Talk: How to Start a Conversation, Keep It Going, Build Networking Skills—and Leave a Positive Impression!*, transformed herself from a shy engineer into a woman who makes a living giving big talks on small talk. The fact that organizations are willing to pay her to teach social skills to their employees speaks to the importance of what may appear to be idle chitchat.

Fine writes that her inability to shoot the breeze caused her to lose a promotion to an equally qualified engineer, for example, and there's no denying the role networking plays in sales and landing jobs.

But in order to network, you first have to be able to chat with strangers, a prospect, Fine says, that fills many people with dread. Fine aims to help readers get over that initial hump before the meaningful conversation kicks in.

It's up to you to break the ice, Fine advises, and not with the trite, "What do you do for a living?"

Instead, she provides a list of openers. Some are inspired ("What advice would you give someone just starting in your business?"), but most are just plain cheesy ("What aroma brings forth a special memory?") or of narrow use ("How are you able to tell if that melon is ripe?"). Best to do as Fine suggests: Remember a handful and dismiss the rest.

Once the ice is broken, Fine writes, keep the talk moving by asking open-ended questions that require your partner to respond with more than a word or two. Don't just say, "How was your weekend?" Instead ask, "What was the best part of your weekend?" Rather than asking if someone is married or if they have children, say, "Tell me about your family."

And once you have someone talking, Fine says, listen instead of thinking about the next thing to say. By paying attention, you'll be able to ask intelligent questions to keep the conversation moving.

Ending a conversation can be as tricky as starting one. Fine writes that one must exit gracefully to leave a positive impression. The best way is to steer the talk back to your original topic, then say honestly why you need to move on. "I want to go talk to the speaker," for example. Or, if you need an emergency exit, simply bow out when a new person joins the group.

The meatiest part of Fine's book is a classification of common behaviors that can kill a conversation. Among easily recognizable types:

*The One-Upper. Doesn't brag first, but always tops others' stories.
*The Monopolizer. Gains control of a conversation and never yields it.
*The Interrupter. Often cuts in because they think they know what you're going to say or they think you're wrong and can't wait to tell you why.
*The Adviser. Most people, Fine says, want empathy and compassion, not solutions.

Among Fine's best tips are how to deal with these so-called conversation criminals, and how not to be one. Advise only when asked, for example, or gently tell an interrupter or one-upper, "This is my story." If you tend to monopolize, limit your story to five minutes.

Also potentially useful is a cheat sheet Fine calls "Fifty Ways to Fuel a Conversation." They include:

*Be the first to say hello.
*Make an extra effort to remember people's names.
*Be able to succinctly tell others what you do.
*Be aware of open and closed body language.
*Seek the opinions of others.
*Look for signs of boredom from your listener.

—February 2, 2010

EPILOGUE
Lifelong COMMUNICATION

You will practice your communication skills your whole life. The skills will help you do things like make friends and find jobs.

Well, here you are. Now you know everything there is to know about communication. You're a pro!

Just kidding. It's impossible to know all there is to know about communicating, because it's something you practice your whole life. But now that you've almost finished this book, you have lots of good ideas and tips to use as you practice.

The best part is that although you can always improve your communication skills, you can never completely fail at communicating. The more you use the tips and ideas in this book, the easier—and more enjoyable—you'll find communicating to be.

Having good communication skills touches every part of your life. It will help you make friends, find jobs, and get the most out of your free time. You'll be able to express your thoughts and feelings to those you love. You'll be able to make small talk with strangers and feel confident in almost any social situation. You'll be better able to gain information and learn about different points of view. And last but not least, good communication is often the only effective way to resolve conflict.

Remember, there's nothing like practice to help boost your communication skills. Look for opportunities to put your skills to work. Start up a conversation with someone you don't know well. Write a letter to your favorite relative. Start reading and contributing to a blog on a topic of interest. You'll find that the more you practice, the more you like communicating and the more skilled you become at it.

GLOSSARY

ARTICULATE: clear and coherent

CONFLICT: a disagreement or dispute between two or more parties, usually with opposing goals

CONVEY: to communicate something

ETIQUETTE: rules of polite behavior

INFLECTION: the way a speaker voices his or her words

MISINTERPRET: to misunderstand the meaning of something

MISSIVE: a letter or written document

PITCH: the highness or lowness of a sound

SOCIAL MEDIA: any of the Internet sites or online tools used for communicating. Examples include websites such as Facebook, Google+, wikis, and Twitter.

TELECOMMUNICATION: communication that takes place over a distance

TONE: a way of speaking that shows a certain emotion or attitude

SELECTED BIBLIOGRAPHY

Benson, T. W., ed. *Speech Communication in the 20th Century*. Carbondale: Southern Illinois University Press, 1985.

Clay, Shirky. *Here Comes Everybody*. New York: Penguin Press, 2008.

Gabbatt, Adam, and Charles Arthur. "Facebook Mail: It Might Kill Gmail, but 'It's Not E-mail.'" *Guardian* (London), November 15, 2010. http://www.guardian .co.uk/technology/2010/nov/15/facebook-mail-gmail-killer-email (August 1, 2011).

Green, John O., and Brant Raney Burleson. *Handbook of Communication and Social Interaction Skills*. Mahwah, NJ: Lawrence Erlbaum Associates, 2003.

Leeds-Hurwitz, W., ed. *Social Approaches to Communication*. New York: Guilford, 1995.

Lenhart, Amanda. *Teens, Cell Phones, and Texting*. Pew Internet & American Life Project. April 20, 2010. http://pewresearch.org/pubs/1572/teens-cell-phones-text-messages (August 1, 2011).

Loechner, Jack. *Teen Media Behavior; Texting, Talking, Socializing, TV Watching, Mobiling*. Center for Media Research. June 23, 2011. http://www .mediapost.com/publications/?fa=Articles.showArticle&art_aid=152661 (August 1, 2011).

Poe, Marshall T. *A History of Communications: Media and Society from the Evolution of Speech to the Internet*. Cambridge: Cambridge University Press, 2011.

Shannon, Victoria. "15 Years of Text Messages, a 'Cultural Phenomenon.'" *New York Times*, December 5, 2007. http://www.nytimes.com/2007/12/05 /technology/05iht-sms.4.8603150.html?pagewanted=all (August 1, 2011).

Shea, Virginia. *The Core Rules of Netiquette*. Albion.com. 2001. http://www .albion.com/netiquette/corerules.html (August 1, 2011).

FURTHER INFORMATION

Carlson, Dale. *Talk: Teen Art of Communication*. Madison, CT: Bick Publishing House, 2006.
  This book for teens offers practical advice and tips to help you improve your communication skills.

DiPiazza, Francesca Davis. *Friend Me!: 600 Years of Social Networking in America*. Minneapolis: Twenty-First Century Books, 2012.
  Learn how Americans have been connecting in imaginative ways throughout history.

Doeden, Matt. *Conflict Resolution Smarts: How to Communicate, Negotiate, Compromise, and More*. Minneapolis: Twenty-First Century Books, 2012.
  Learn more about how to put your communication skills to work to successfully resolve conflict.

List of Chat Acronyms and Text Message Shorthand
  http://www.netlingo.com/acronyms.php
  Look up hundreds of texting abbreviations in this list from NetLingo.

Post Senning, Cindy. *Teen Manners: From Malls to Meals to Messaging and Beyond*. New York: HarperCollins, 2007.
  Get tips on texting, letter writing, and more in this manners guide for teens written by the granddaughter of famous manners writer Emily Post.

Roza, Greg. *Great Networking Skills*. New York: Rosen, 2008.
  Learn how to put your communications skills to work to help you land a job. This guide is for teens.

Social Networking Sites: Safety Tips for Tweens and Teens
  http://www.ftc.gov/bcp/edu/pubs/consumer/tech/tec14.shtm
  Find tips from the Federal Trade Commission for guarding your privacy and safety online at this site for teens.

Sommers, Michael A. *Great Interpersonal Skills*. New York: Rosen, 2008.
  This guide offers practical advice for using communication skills to get along in the workplace.

TeensHealth: 5 Ways to Ace a Job Interview
http://kidshealth.org/teen/school_jobs/jobs/tips_interview.html#cat20180
Want to ace your next job interview? Check out this site for some great tips
on how to impress your future employer.

"Texting May Be Taking a Toll on Teenagers"
http://www.nytimes.com/2009/05/26/health/26teen.html?_r=1
Some doctors and educators are concerned that teens are texting too much.
This article discusses the problem and some of the potential dangers.

Woods, Mary B., and Michael Woods. *Ancient Communication Technology: From
Hieroglyphics to Scrolls.* Minneapolis: Twenty-First Century Books, 2011.
Read about the communication tools and techniques used by ancient
people, and learn how ancient communication set the stage for our own
modern communication technology.

LERNER

SOURCE

Expand learning beyond the printed book. Download free, complementary
educational resources for this book from our website, www.lerneresource.com.

INDEX

ABOUT THE AUTHOR

Sandy Donovan has written many books for teens, including *Volunteering Smarts: How to Find Opportunities, Create a Positive Experience, and More* in the USA Today Teen Wise Guides series. She has a bachelor's degree in journalism and political science and a master's degree in public policy. She lives in Minneapolis with her husband, two sons, and a dog named Fred.